D1318500

Circus Counting

illustrated by Ronald Fabec
written by Dandi

One Ringmaster shouts out loud,
"Start the circus! Hush the crowd!"

Look up high! Now look still higher!
Two men walk the tightrope wire.

In *three* spotlights, on *three* stairs,
You can see *three* dancing bears.

Four fire eaters with flaming swords,
Accept applause as their rewards.

Five fierce tigers leap through fire.
Crack the whip, and they leap higher.

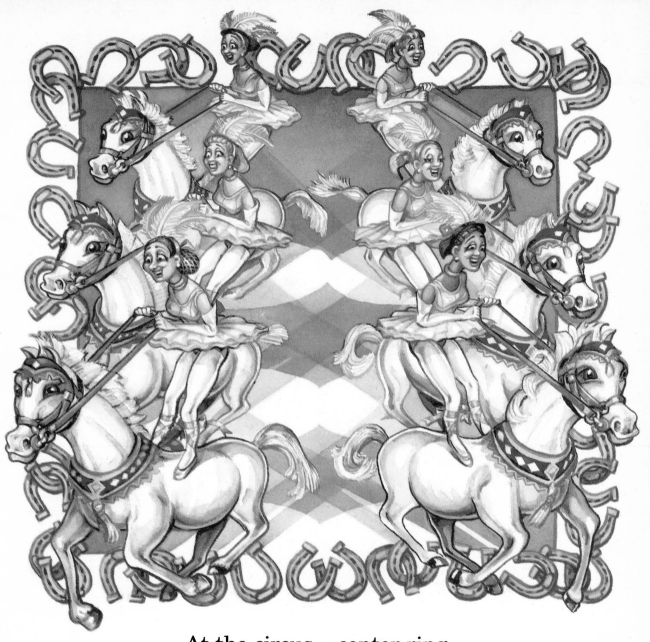

At the circus – center ring,
Six white horses galloping.

Seven monkeys, *seven* balloons,
Dance to organ grinder tunes.

Eight elephants in parade,
Form an elephant brigade.

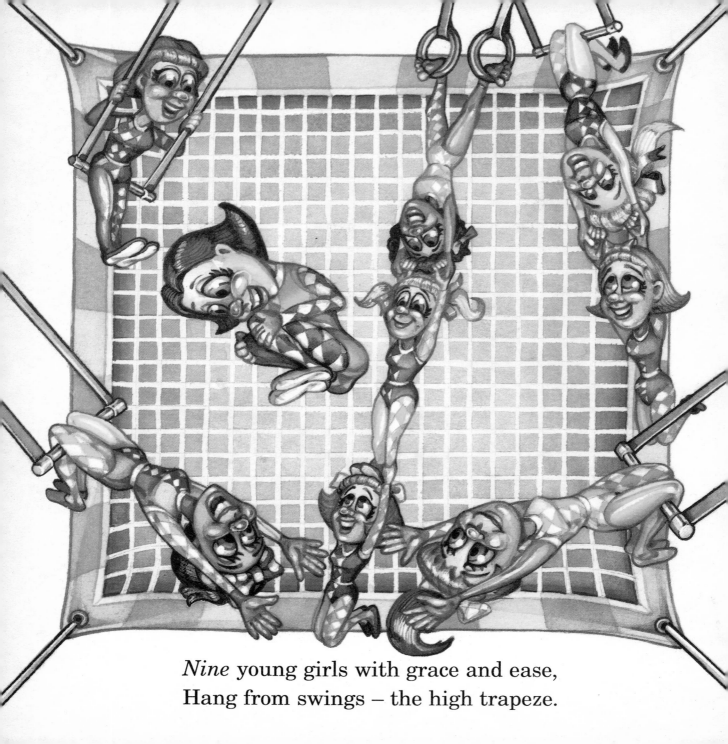

Nine young girls with grace and ease,
Hang from swings – the high trapeze.

Don't forget a single clown, when the circus comes to town.
Count them now, and you will see, *ten* tall clowns on bended knee.

Ten clowns wave good-bye to you.
Circus time is almost through.

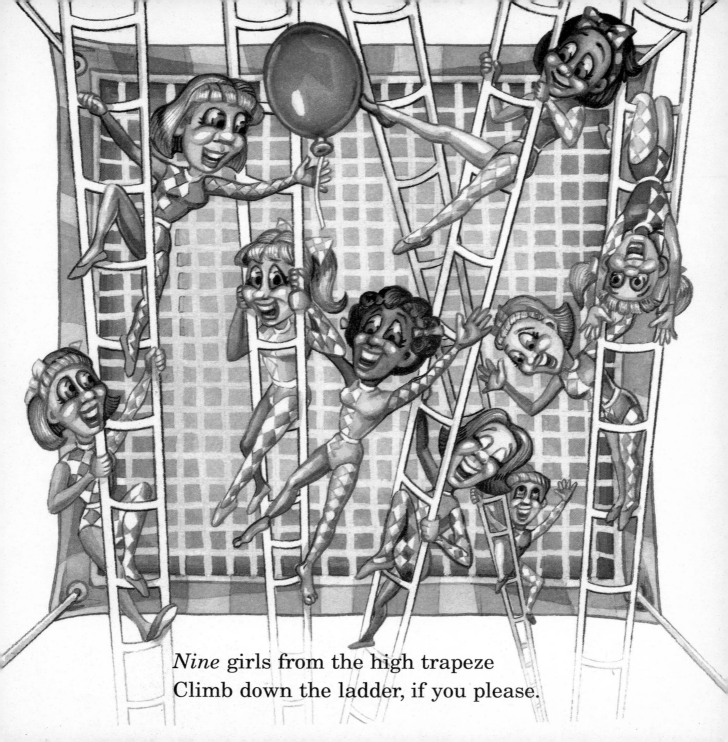

Nine girls from the high trapeze
Climb down the ladder, if you please.

Eight gray elephants, *eight* big hunks,
Start to pack their *eight* pink trunks.

Seven monkeys, off they went!
Balloons float up the circus tent.

Six white horses say goodnight,
Just in time to eat a bite.

Five striped tigers once again
Saunter to their tiger den.

Our *four* fire eaters quit.
Time to drink a little bit.

Three brown bears – no time to lose –
Try to shed their dancing shoes.

Off the tightrope jump *two* men!
In the net – then out again.